3.89

INTERIM SITE

SHORT TERM
LOAN

VALENTINE'S DAY
Stories and Poems

Edited by Caroline Feller Bauer
Illustrated by Blanche L. Sims

HarperCollins*Publishers*

FOR PETER

My valentine for 30 years

Valentine's Day: *Stories and Poems*
Text copyright © 1993 by Caroline Feller Bauer
Illustrations copyright © 1993 by Blanche L. Sims
HarperCollins Children's Books, a division of
HarperCollins Publishers,
10 East 53rd Street, New York, NY 10022.
1   2   3   4   5   6   7   8   9   10   ❖
First Edition

Library of Congress Cataloging-in-Publication Data
Valentine's day : stories and poems / edited by Caroline Feller Bauer ;
illustrated by Blanche L. Sims
    p.   cm.
   Summary: A collection of stories, poems, and activities by a variety of
authors, on the theme of Valentine's Day.
    ISBN 0-06-020823-6. — ISBN 0-06-020824-4 (lib. bdg.)
    1. Valentine's Day—Literary collections. [1. Valentine's Day—
Literary collections.] I. Bauer, Caroline Feller. II. Sims, Blanche, ill.
PZ5.V25 1993   91-37641
810.8' 033—dc20   CIP
                                                              AC

ACKNOWLEDGMENTS

Every effort has been made to trace ownership of all copyrighted material and to secure the necessary permissions to reprint these selections. In the event of any question arising as to the use of any material, the editor and the publisher, while expressing regret for any inadvertent error, will be happy to make the necessary correction in future printings. Thanks are due to the following for permission to reprint the copyrighted materials below:

Atheneum Publishers, an imprint of Macmillan Publishing Company, for "Conversation Hearts" from *All the Day Long* by Nina Payne. Copyright © 1973 by Nina Payne. / Atheneum Publishers, an imprint of Macmillan Publishing Company, for "Short Love Poem," ". . . . And Then the Prince Knelt Down and Tried to Put the Glass Slipper on Cinderella's Foot," and "The Lizzie Pitofsky Poem" from *If I Were in Charge of the World and Other Worries* by Judith Viorst. Copyright © 1981 by Judith Viorst. / Bradbury Press, an affiliate of Macmillan, Inc., for "Ellie's Valentine" from *A Blue-Eyed Daisy* by Cynthia Rylant. Copyright © 1985 by Cynthia Rylant. / Curtis Brown Ltd., for "A Valentine To My Puppy" from *Cricket* magazine. Copyright © 1992 by Jane Yolen. / Katherine H. Dent for "When You Send a Valentine" by Mildred J. Hill from *Away We Go! 100 Poems for the Very Young* compiled by Catherine Schaeffer McEwen. Copyright © 1956 by Catherine Schaefer McEwen, Thomas Y. Crowell Company. / Dutton Children's Books, a division of Penguin Books USA Inc., for "The Cat-King's Daughter" from *The Town Cats and Other Tales* by Lloyd Alexander. Copyright © 1979 by Lloyd Alexander. / Farrar, Straus & Giroux, Inc., for "two friends" from *Spin a Soft Black Song* by Nikki Giovanni. Copyright © 1971, 1985 by Nikki Giovanni. / HarperCollins Publishers, for "Love Don't Mean" from *Honey, I Love* by Eloise Greenfield. Copyright © 1978 by Eloise Greenfield. / HarperCollins Publishers, for "X X X X X" from *Zoomrimes* by Sylvia Cassedy. Copyright © 1991 by the Estate of Sylvia Cassedy. / HarperCollins Publishers, for "I Like Bugs" from *Near the Window Tree* by Karla Kuskin. Copyright © 1975 by Karla Kuskin. / HarperCollins Publishers, for "Valentine" from *Skip Around the Year* by Aileen Fisher. Copyright © 1967 by Aileen Fisher. / HarperCollins Publishers, for "Hug Me." Copyright © 1977 by Patti Stren. / Michael Patrick Hearn, for "The Valentine." Copyright © 1993 by Michael Patrick Hearn. / Hill and Wang, a division of Farrar, Straus & Giroux, Inc., for "Love Tight" from *Afrodisia* by Ted Joans. Copyright © 1970 by Ted Joans. / Houghton Mifflin Company, for "Here It Is" from *Street Talk* by Ann Turner. Copyright © 1986 by Ann Turner. / Bobbi Katz, for "Private Valentines." Copyright © 1993 by Bobbi Katz. / Alfred A. Knopf, Inc. for "Poem" from *The Dream Keeper and Other Poems* by Langston Hughes. Copyright 1932 and renewed 1960 by Langston Hughes. / Ruth Krauss, for "Making Sandwich-Kisses." Copyright © 1981 by Ruth Krauss. / Karla Kuskin, for "The Porcupine" from *Cricket* magazine. Copyright © 1974 by Karla Kuskin. / Lothrop, Lee and Shepard Books (a division of William Morrow & Company, Inc.) for the second half of the poem "Love Song" from *Eats* by Arnold Adoff. Copyright © 1979 by Arnold Adoff. / Gina Maccoby Literary Agency for "Giraffes" from *Yellow Butter Purple Jelly Red Jam Black Bread* by Mary Ann Hoberman. Copyright © 1981 by Mary Ann Hoberman. / McIntosh and Otis, Inc., for "A Valentine's Day Poem." Copyright © 1991 by Miriam Chaikin. / Gordon Parks, for "You Are." Copyright © 1971 by Gordon Parks. / Linda G. Paulsen, for "February." Copyright © 1993 by Linda G. Paulsen. / Marian Reiner, Permissions Consultant, for "Be My Non-Valentine" from *A Sky Full of Poems* by Eve Merriam. Copyright © 1964, 1970, 1973 by Eve Merriam. / Marian Reiner, Permissions Consultant, for "When." Copyright © 1993 by Eve Merriam.

Contents

Conversation Hearts   *Nina Payne*   3

Valentines   *Aileen Fisher*   4

Love Don't Mean   *Eloise Greenfield*   5

The Porcupine   *Karla Kuskin*   6

Making Sandwich-Kisses   *Ruth Krauss*   7

Hug Me, a Story   *Patti Stren*   9

Short Love Poem   *Judith Viorst*   13

February   *Linda G. Paulsen*   14

Love Tight   *Ted Joans*   15

Be My Non-Valentine   *Eve Merriam*   16

Private Valentines   *Bobbi Katz*   17

When You Send a Valentine   *Mildred J. Hill*   18

Ellie's Valentine, a Story   *Cynthia Rylant*   21

A Valentine To My Puppy   *Jane Yolen*   37

Here It Is   *Ann Turner*   38

I like bugs   *Karla Kuskin*   40

two friends   *Nikki Giovanni*   41

Poem   *Langston Hughes*   42

X X X X X X   *Sylvia Cassedy*   43

Make a Gift for Your Valentine   44

You are   *Gordon Parks*   46

When   *Eve Merriam*   47

. . . And Then the Prince Knelt Down
    and Tried to Put the Glass Slipper
    on Cinderella's Foot   *Judith Viorst*   48

The Cat-King's Daughter, a Story
    Lloyd Alexander   51

A Valentine's Day Poem   *Miriam Chaikin*   71

My Valentine   *Robert Louis Stevenson*   72

Giraffes   *Mary Ann Hoberman*   73

From Love Song   *Arnold Adoff*   74

Make Yourself, and Your Valentine,
    a Holiday Sweet   75

Does She Love Me? Does He Love Me?   76

Did you eever, iver, over   *Traditional*   79

The Lizzie Pitofsky Poem   *Judith Viorst*   80

The Valentine   *Michael Patrick Hearn*   82

"I Love You" Around the World   84

SOMETHING TO READ   86

INDEX   89

VALENTINE'S DAY

Stories and Poems

Conversation Hearts

NINA PAYNE

In February, bring them home,
pink, yellow, lavender
and lime pastels
BE MINE   I'M YOURS
to be read by the tongue
that licks the chalk
and tastes what it spells.

I'll give you a boxful,
tasting of daphne, lupin,
mint and columbine;
a mouthful of secrets,
lovelier than whispers,
dear ones, friends
I'M YOURS   BE MINE

Valentines

AILEEN FISHER

I gave a hundred Valentines.
A hundred, did I say?
I gave a *thousand* Valentines
one cold and wintry day.

I didn't put my name on them
or any other words,
because my Valentines were seeds
for February birds.

4

Love Don't Mean

ELOISE GREENFIELD

Love don't mean all that kissing
Like on television
Love means Daddy
Saying keep your mama company
    till I get back
And me doing it

The Porcupine

KARLA KUSKIN

A porcupine looks somewhat silly,
He also is extremely quilly
And if he shoots a quill at you
Run fast
Or you'll be quilly too.

I would not want a porcupine
To be my loving valentine.

Making Sandwich-Kisses

RUTH KRAUSS

For instance, when your mother has been out a long time and she comes home and you run and kiss her, and your father runs and kisses her too, and then everybody kisses each other—that's sandwich-kisses.

Hug Me

PATTI STREN

Elliot Kravitz was not like other porcupines, who were quite content having quills and being left alone.

Elliot was not content. He wanted a friend. A friend to talk to, a friend to play with and tell his best secrets to, but mostly a friend to hug.

All his friends told him, "Hey, Elliot! It's really great having quills!!

"No one bothers us. We always get to be first in line. And we never have to share our ice-cream cones. No one ever comes near a porcupine!"

But Elliot rather liked being with people. He never really minded sharing his ice-cream cone, even if it was a double-scoop, chocolate chip cone with sprinkles on top.

Elliot longed for a friend. You see, there was one thing he wanted more than anything else in the world . . . A BIG, TIGHT HUG. The other porcupines wouldn't hug him. It's too hard, they said, to hug someone with quills.

So Elliot spent a lot of his time hugging telephone poles, parking meters, and traffic lights.

After a while, Elliot got tired of hugging telephone poles, parking meters, and traffic lights. They really didn't make him feel very good.

During the day, he continued to hug things. And then at night, in bed, Elliot would dream about having a real friend who would hug back.

One morning, he got out of bed and said, "Enough is enough. No more hugging parking meters, traffic lights, and telephone poles. I want a friend to hug! A friend who will hug me back."

Elliot decided to disguise himself as a birthday present. People love birthday presents. Maybe someone who loved birthday presents would want to be his friend.

When it was Christmas, Elliot put lights around each quill and rented himself out as the first walking Christmas tree.

Everyone loved to look at him, but no one ever wanted to touch him. He never got hugged.

By this time, Elliot was very angry and upset. "I'll get even," he said. "I'll put erasers on each of my quills and wipe everyone out!"

Then he said to himself, "Elliot, you're being silly. There's nothing you can do."

And then he said, out loud for everyone to hear, "I GIVE UP! I don't need anybody. I'm going to the forest where I can be alone and no one will ever find me!"

In the forest, Elliot found himself a quiet, grassy spot under a tree. He sat hugging his knees. "You give up what?" a little voice said. Elliot turned around and saw another porcupine facing him.

"What's your name?" she said.

"Elliot Kravitz," said Elliot Kravitz. "What's yours?"

"Thelma Claypits," said Thelma Claypits. "What are you doing here?" she said.

"I'm here because nobody wants to hug me."

"I'll hug you," she said.

"You will?" said Elliot.

"Sure," said Thelma.

"But I'm a porcupine," said Elliot.

"What do you think I am?" she said, pointing to her quills. "Lets hug."

And they tried . . . slowly, carefully, very gently, they hugged.

Elliot smiled.

"This is nice," he thought to himself.

Short Love Poem

JUDITH VIORST

It's hard to love
The tallest girl
When you're the shortest guy,
For every time
You try to look
Your true love in the eye
You see
Her bellybutton.

13

February

LINDA G. PAULSEN

February's dreary;
It rains for days at a time.
The wind blows,
Then it snows;
The streets are covered with grime.

February's weary;
We long for Spring, and sun.
Thank goodness, I say,
For Valentine's Day;
Or the month would be empty of fun.

Love Tight

TED JOANS

Place your hand
Into my hand and
Open your mouth
Wide as my mouth
And close your eyes
As tight as you can
Then imagine we
Both are two
Lions in love
Forever

Be My Non-Valentine

EVE MERRIAM

I have searched my Thesaurus through
to find a synonym for you;
here are some choice words that may do:

you're a hoddy-doddy, a dizzard, a ninny, a dolt,
a booby, a looby, a fribble, a gowk,
a nonny, a nizy, a nincompoop,
a churl, a scrimp, a knag, a trapes,
a lubber, a marplot, an oaf, a droil,
a mopus, a flat, a muff, a doit,
a mugwump, a dimwit, a flunkey, a swab,
a bane, a murrain, a malkin, a pox,
a sloven, a slammerkin, a draggel tail,
frumpery, scrannel, and kickshaw, too!

Private Valentines

BOBBI KATZ

In gray February
my tongue tingles
with little cinnamon fires.
One by one
tiny red hearts
burn quietly inside my mouth.
Each one a separate valentine—
private.
From me . . .
to me.

When You Send a Valentine

MILDRED J. HILL

When you send a valentine—
That's the time for fun!
Push it underneath the door,
Ring the bell and run, run, run!
Ring the bell and run!

Ellie's Valentine

CYNTHIA RYLANT

One day in February there came a snow into the mountains that was so big even the old ones couldn't remember any storm ever outdoing it.

It began secretly during the night, and when Ellie's mother called them all out of bed the next morning and they got a look outside, the first thing the girls wondered was if school would be called off.

They turned on their radio to listen for news of the county schools. But the radio announcer said that, as far as he knew, all schools were open. The county superintendent had not called.

Ellie kicked the bottom of the refrigerator. But her sisters squealed with delight.

Okey said, "Well, praise the Lord. I couldn't have stood staying cooped up with six women in this house." Then he went outside to check on Bullet.

Ellie slowly pulled on her clothes. The real reason she didn't want to go to school was not the staying at home. She didn't want to go because it was Valentine's Day, and she couldn't bear it if no boy gave her a special valentine. She had already considered being sick for the day, but the thought of staying around Okey and her mother and their squawking had changed her mind.

She knew why her sisters were so happy to be going to school. They all had boyfriends and they knew something special was waiting for them.

Nothing was waiting for Ellie but disgrace.

The snowplows had been through during the night, so the only real trouble they had walking to the bus stop was getting out of their yard. Huge drifts lay alongside the road, and the trees suffered under heavy sleeves of snow. It was still dark, for the sun hadn't risen yet, but the snow served as some illumination. The girls tramped out to the stop.

Their bus stop was one of the few that had a

shelter. Just a wooden building with three walls and no front, but it kept the wind off on bitter mornings.

This morning, though, the snow had been shoved by the plow right up to the shelter and partly into it. About four feet high. Enough to discourage anybody with cold feet and legs from trying to dig through.

"Oh, no!" cried Eunice. She had taken an especially long time to arrange her hair at home. Standing in the road, waiting for the bus in the wet snow and wind, would ruin her, even with the scarf she was wearing.

"My *hair*!" she cried.

The other girls, less concerned than Eunice about hair matters, ignored her.

Eventually more riders showed up. Judy and Joseph White. C. E. and Cathy Connor. Sonny Mills.

The bus was going to be late. They had already figured that out. So they all hopped and jumped and danced and whistled and whooped and crowed and giggled and shivered and

23

moaned in the road. Waiting for County Bus 53.

And just when they were beginning to give up, just when Ellie was starting to take hope that she could avoid this year's Valentine's Day, the wide thick headlights of the bus came over the top of the half-moon hill and everyone (except her) cheered and stamped, then finally climbed on. She was last.

The driver, Mr. Danner, nodded to each of them. He wasn't usually friendly. Just picked them up and dropped them off. Did his job. Sometimes, though, he'd blow the horn a few times and wait in the road a minute if someone

was missing from a bus stop. He'd wait to see if the late one would come puffing over the hill. Or if the rider lived next to the road, Mr. Danner would look toward the front window of the house for a sign of whether someone was coming or not.

Some bus drivers didn't bother to honk or to wait. Ellie knew that, so she decided she liked Mr. Danner.

The bus lumbered along the snowy road on its way toward the elementary school to drop off Ellie and the kids through eighth grade before it headed on out to Monroe County High School

with the rest. Ellie sat alone. She looked out the window and silently cursed Valentine's Day and boys and school and her sisters and all that made her plain miserable.

The next stop was at Willie Peters' house. All six kids were at that stop, hopping and blowing. At each stop it looked like almost everybody was making it to school, even the ones who had to walk down off the mountains.

When they came to Blue Jay Six Hill, Ellie wished in her heart the bus might not make it. Might just slide all the way down the hill and back the way it had come. But even Blue Jay Six Hill let her down, and they kept going.

Ellie could just see what would happen at school. They'd make some stupid little valentine to give to their parents or Someone Special the way they always did. Then the boys would sneak around and slide their valentines under some girl's desk top. And Ellie would clean out her desk at the end of the day and come up empty-handed.

She decided she'd make a valentine for

26

Bullet. Let him chew it up good when she got home.

The bus began slowing down for a stop. Ellie looked out the window to see who was waiting at this one, then she realized there was no bus stop on this stretch of the road. Everybody else did, too.

"What's going on?"

Mr. Danner let the bus idle a few seconds, then shifted, pulled the emergency brake and shut off the engine.

The loud heater stopped blowing and the sudden silence scared them all.

"It's a tree!" someone in front shouted.

Ellie jumped up to get a look with everyone else. Sure enough, it was a tree. A big tree, an old tree, a tree too tired to carry all the snow. And it had cracked and fallen across the road, waiting for County Bus 53 to find it.

Hallelujah, Ellie thought.

Mr. Danner climbed off and stood outside, speculating.

Finally he climbed back on.

27

"Well, kids," he said, "looks like we gotta hike."

"Hike?"

"No other way to get around it. Can't back up on this mountain, that's for sure. And that tree's not going anywhere. We'll have to walk to the Meadors' on up the road."

Everybody started talking, giggling, full of excitement. Except, of course, the high-school girls, like Eunice, whose plans were falling to ruin.

Ellie couldn't believe her luck.

"Okay now, button up. Gloves on, you little ones. You big ones, too, for that matter. Leave your books and lunches on the bus. We'll get 'em later."

Mr. Danner led the way out the door. And all twenty-eight of them followed. The kindergartners circled around the bus driver, holding each other's hands, and the group started walking.

A little boy fell at once. Mr. Danner picked him up and muttered something about slick cowboy boots.

Laughter and talk echoed from them into the woods. Ellie was thrilled. Not only did it look like she was going to avoid humiliation at school—she was actually having a good time. A real adventure in the life of Ellie Farley. Wait until Okey heard about hiking in the dark morning, stranded, hungry (she'd stretch it a little), searching for shelter.

He'd be impressed.

After about ten minutes of walking, though, some of the little ones started asking exactly how far it was to the Meadors'. Even the big ones didn't know for sure if it was just around the next curve, or the next, or the next . . .

Then, after about fifteen minutes of hard walking on that icy road in the snow and wind with no house in sight, the laughter and the talk got thinner. After about twenty minutes, it stopped. And Ellie was breathing hard, her throat was feeling cold deep down inside, and her eyes were watering up.

Someone in the group of kindergartners sobbed. That's all they needed, all the little ones.

29

They started sniffling, one by one, and before anybody was ready for it, they were wailing.

Ellie decided disgrace, shame and humiliation were all better than what the hike was turning into.

Mr. Danner tried to give the small ones hugs and words of encouragement, but there were eight of them and only one of him.

"My feet hurt," one boy cried, tears streaming warm down his cold, red face.

Everyone waited to see what Mr. Danner would do.

"Okay, Bobby," he answered. "If your feet hurt, let me give you a lift."

To Ellie's amazement, he lifted the child onto his shoulders.

"Now, let's try again, kids. Just a little further on." He smiled at them, patted Bobby's legs and went on.

But another little one started crying. And, to everyone's surprise, one of the high-school boys caught up with her and lifted her into his arms.

30

It made Ellie almost wish she were five years old.

And as they all struggled along, the smaller ones grew so cold and tired that eventually, one by one, they were each picked up by someone larger.

Everyone was silent. Ellie was sad. And so cold. Worst morning of her life.

Those who were carrying the smaller children struggled not to slip and fall, but some fell anyway. And the two would go down together. Some of the small ones could laugh it off and start all over. But others cried.

Still, somehow, amid the falls, and the

bruises, the throats sore from the wind and the throbbing, aching fingers—somehow in spite of all this, they made that last turn and saw the Meador house up ahead.

Shouts went up. Ellie whooped like her daddy. They whistled and jumped up and down and hugged each other.

They had made it.

The planks of the Meador porch echoed with the stamping of tired feet, then the wooden door opened wide. The warmth of a home eased the coldness from each face as the twenty-eight passengers plus one bus driver dragged inside.

"Oh, you poor children!" Mrs. Meador said as she moved to each one, framing their cheeks with her plump hands. "God love your bones!"

She and her husband and her son James, who had long before given up on the bus and trudged back home, helped pull off scarfs and mittens and coats and boots. When he came to Ellie, James seemed shy but pleased to have her in his house. He had never quite gotten over the thrill of her Christmas cookies.

"Whew!" Ellie said. "Talk about cold!" James took her things to be laid out to dry, and she huddled on the big braided rug in front of the fireplace with everyone else.

Eunice was feeling her damp, straggly hair, a little pout on her face.

"Shoot, Eun," Ellie said. "Don't worry about it. I bet when Keith Evans finds out you didn't make it to school, he'll hike himself all the way to our house."

Eunice just pouted harder, so Ellie ignored her.

The Meadors were giving out cups of sugary warm tea, and as the kids thawed, they got noisier.

Even Ellie began to feel exuberant again. She had escaped Valentine's Day. And she and all the rest had accomplished something brave and wonderful. And, for this morning, she deeply loved Mr. Danner.

James came up with a cup of tea for her and one for himself and squeezed in to sit beside her.

"Some valentine, huh?" he commented.

Ellie sputtered and splashed some of the tea on her pants.

"You can say that again!"

"You hungry?" he asked.

"Huh?"

"Hungry?"

"Well . . . sure. I guess," she answered.

"Come on then."

She got up and followed him through the living room, up the stairs to the second floor and into a bedroom.

"This your room?" she asked.

"Uh-huh." He started rummaging through a bureau drawer.

The room had pictures of airplanes covering every wall. Ellie had never seen so many pictures of airplanes.

"You like planes?" she asked.

"Uh-huh." He shut the drawer and started digging into another one.

"I've never seen so many planes," she said, walking all around the room and looking at some of them up close.

"Found it!"

She turned to look at James. And in his hand was a wide, flat box that looked like it might hold handkerchiefs.

He walked over to her and opened the lid. Inside were a Christmas bell, painted red and white, and a stocking, painted pink and yellow with blue trim.

Ellie looked at him.

"You saved these two cookies since Christmas?"

James grinned. "Yep."

Ellie shook her head in disbelief.

"Want one?" he asked.

Ellie grinned.

"They're not *rotten?*"

"Heck, no. This room's so cold most of the time, they could probably keep till June."

Ellie chose the stocking. She bit into it. It was good. A little tough, but good.

"Why'd you save them?"

James shrugged his shoulders and looked shyly away.

"Just liked 'em, that's all. Wanted to make them last."

Ellie sat down on the rug with him and finished her cookie. They drank their tea and talked about airplanes and war and dogs and the hike Ellie had just made.

At home later that night, it occurred to Ellie that God couldn't have made a more perfect Valentine's Day.

A Valentine
To My Puppy

JANE YOLEN

I think of you, I think of bones,
The toothmarked cords of telephones,
The loose ends of upholstered chairs,
A slipper with the heel in tears,
A rubber ball, a mangled sock,
The splintered mass of baby's block.
These valentines you leave around
Signed: "Love from me, your favorite hound."

I do love you, you know, despite
The signature of doggy bite.
And I look forward to the days
You show *your* love in other ways.

Here It Is

ANN TURNER

I love food
pizza-pepper plucking
at my throat
(hey-hot! hey-hot!),
fizzy Coke tickling
my nose (sssz-bam! sssz-bam!)
and a hamburger with all
the trimmings
slip-sliding out
when you munch down.

I love food
late at night
a crispy-crackly pack
of Doritos,
a fistful of Cheez Whiz,
a Twinkie soft and slinky.

But most I love
sitting at the table
with Ma frying bacon,
her steps whisp-shushing
back and forth, humming
(you can't *make* eggs right
without humming)
and she says, "Ben,
here it is,"

and there it is.

I like bugs

KARLA KUSKIN

I like bugs.
I kiss them
And I give them hugs.

two friends

NIKKI GIOVANNI

lydia and shirley have
two pierced ears and
two bare ones
five pigtails
two pairs of sneakers
two berets
two smiles
one necklace
one bracelet
lots of stripes and
one good friendship

41

Poem

LANGSTON HUGHES

I loved my friend.
He went away from me.
There's nothing more to say.
The poem ends,
Soft as it began—
I loved my friend.

X X X X X X

SYLVIA CASSEDY

I sealed this note with kisses—
six in all—
each one a little cross of wings,
like vanes on a swinging windmill
or a wooden whirligig.
Then, as soon as they are posted,
just you wait and see!
The wings will all start spinning,
and fly my note to you
from me.

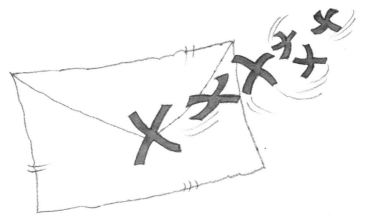

Make a Gift for Your Valentine

Make your own clay Valentine pendant to give to your Valentine friend.

You need:
1 cup cornstarch
2 cups baking soda
1 ¼ cups cold water

How to:
Mix all ingredients together and place on low heat, stirring constantly. When the mixture looks like moist mashed potatoes, put it on a plate and cover it with a damp cloth until it is cool enough to handle. Now the clay is ready to shape. (Leftover clay can be stored in a sealed plastic bag.)

Mold the clay into the shape of a heart. Pierce a hole in the clay so that the heart can be worn as a pendant. Let the heart dry until it is hard. Paint your name and your friend's name on the pendant, or paste a piece of paper that has a name or decoration on it on the heart.

You are

GORDON PARKS

You are
all there is,
Has been
       and
Will be.
So
What you are,
Have become
       and
Shall be
       is
Through your love
What I am.

When

EVE MERRIAM

When fire's freezing cold,
when snow is boiling hot,
when birds forget to sing,
I'll still forget you not.

When every story ends,
when spring does not renew,
when all the clocks have stopped,
then I'll stop loving you.

. . . And Then the Prince Knelt Down and Tried to Put the Glass Slipper on Cinderella's Foot

JUDITH VIORST

I really didn't notice that he had a funny nose.
And he certainly looked better all dressed up in
    fancy clothes.
He's not nearly as attractive as he seemed the
    other night.
So I think I'll just pretend that this glass slipper
    feels too tight.

48

The Cat-King's Daughter

LLOYD ALEXANDER

Princess Elena of Ventadorn loved Raimond, Count of Albiclair. However, as much as the two young people had set their hearts on marrying, so King Hugo, father of Elena, had set his against it.

"That lute plucker?" cried Hugo. "That verse scribbler? He should be out hunting, or carousing; or invading the next province, like any self-respecting nobleman. Worse yet, his estates are unspeakably small and his fortune intolerably smaller. In short, the fellow's worthless."

"That's your opinion," said Elena. "Not mine."

"Indeed it is," replied Hugo. "And whose judgement better than the King's?"

"You say that about everything," declared Elena. "Because pickled herrings happen to give you colic, you've forbidden them to all your subjects. Because holidays bore you, the kingdom has none. You can't abide cats, so you've

51

made it a crime to keep one, to feed one, or even to shelter a kitten."

"So it should be," retorted the King. "Cats! Impudent beasts! They won't fetch or carry. They wave their tails in your face. They stare at you bold as brass, then stick out their tongues and go to washing themselves."

"I call that clean," said Elena, "hardly criminal."

"Worse than criminal, it's disrespectful," snapped the King. "Disobedient and insolent, like headstrong girls who don't take no for an answer."

So, the more Elena urged his consent to marry Raimond, the more stubbornly the King refused. Instead, he sent word for other suitors properly—and profitably—qualified to present themselves at court; and he locked Princess Elena in her chambers, there to receive them and choose one to be her husband.

Princess Elena matched her father in strength of will; and no sooner was the door bolted after her than she determined to escape and make her way to Raimond as quickly as she could. But her chambers in the North Tower of the palace were too high for her to jump from the casement. Since King Hugo disliked ivy, none grew along the steep walls; and, without a handhold, the stones were too smooth for her to clamber down. Though she pulled the sheets and coverlets from her bed and knotted them together, this makeshift ladder barely reached halfway to the courtyard below. The more she cast about for other means, the more clearly she saw there were none. At last, she threw herself on the couch, crying in rage and frustration.

Then she heard a voice say:

"Princess, why do you weep?"

At her feet sat a tabby cat, honey-colored with dark stripes, thin as a mackerel, every rib showing under her bedraggled coat. Though she looked more used to alleys than palaces, she seemed quite at ease amid the soft carpets and embroidered draperies. Instead of crouching fearfully, she studied the Princess with bold curiosity through emerald eyes much the same hue as those of Elena.

"If I had satin cushions to sleep on," said the cat, "and goosedown quilts, and silken bedspreads, I wouldn't be in such a hurry to leave them."

"A cat?" exclaimed the Princess, for a moment forgetting her predicament. "But there are no cats in the palace."

"Well, there is one now," answered the cat, "and my name is Margot." She then explained how she had slipped through the palace gate that morning while the guard was changing.

"But why?" asked Elena. "You must know how my father feels about cats. And here, of all places—"

"Where better?" said Margot. "Who'd expect to find a cat under King Hugo's very nose? I was hoping for a warm cubbyhole to hide in, and a few leftovers from the kitchen. But once inside the palace, I had to dodge so many courtiers, and got so turned around in the hallways and staircases, I was glad for the first open door I came to."

"Poor creature," said Elena, venturing to stroke the cat, "you're hardly more than skin and bones."

"Thanks to your father's decree," said Margot.

"Luckily, some people have better sense than to pay it any mind. Now and again, a housewife puts out some scraps or a saucer of milk. For the rest, we forage as best we can. King Hugo hasn't made life easy for a cat."

"Nor a princess," replied Elena, glad for the chance to unburden her heart by telling her troubles to Margot.

After listening attentively to the account, the cat thoughtfully preened her whiskers for several moments, then said:

"We cats won't abide doing what we're forced to do, so I understand your feelings. But I doubt very much you can be made to marry against your will. King Hugo may rant and rave; but practically speaking, he surely won't tie you hand and foot and drag you by the hair to the wedding ceremony. A bride, kicking and screaming? Hardly flattering for a husband-to-be."

"True," Elena admitted. "But I love Raimond and want him for my husband. How shall I make my father change his mind? What if no one else claimed my hand? I'll make sure they don't! I'll paste a wart on the end of my nose, and paint myself a mustache. That should be discouraging enough."

"Princess," said the cat, "your beauty is too great to hide, no matter what you do."

"I won't eat," said Elena. "I'll starve myself."

"Be sensible," said the cat. "Your father need only wait. Your hunger will soon get the best of you."

"I'm afraid you're right," Elena agreed. "Very well, when these suitors come, I'll refuse to see them. Let them break down the door! I shan't speak a word to them. There's nothing else I can do."

"Yes, there is," said the cat. "What I have in mind might even help us cats as well as you. First, you must do as I ask now. Then, tomorrow, you must stay hidden under the couch. Be warned, however: What happens may bring you joy—or it may break your heart."

Princess Elena could not imagine herself more heartbroken than she was. And so, despite the cat's warning, she willingly agreed. As

Margot instructed her, she combed and brushed the cat until the fur was as soft and glistening as her own tresses. Then she draped the cat in one of her silken scarves and tied a necklace of pearls at Margot's waist. She set a diamond bracelet as a crown on Margot's head; and adorned the cat's paws and tail with the finest rings of emeralds, rubies, and sapphires.

Next morning, King Hugo came to order his daughter to make ready for her suitors. But instead of Elena, out of sight beneath the couch, he found Margot, royally attired, comfortably stretched out amid the satin pillows.

"What's this?" roared the King. "What's this cat doing here? Scat! Scat!" He shouted for Elena, but she never stirred. Before the King thought to search the chambers, Margot glanced calmly at him and, in a voice resembling that of Elena, said:

"Father, how is it that you don't recognize your own daughter?"

At this, King Hugo stared speechless and his head began to whirl. Seeing nothing of Princess

Elena in the apartments, he could only believe that she had indeed turned into a cat overnight. Then his bewilderment changed to anger and he shook a finger under Margot's nose:

"You've done it on purpose," he cried, "out of sheer stubbornness, to vex and spite me! How you managed it, I don't know. But I command you: Turn yourself back again! Immediately!"

"That," said Margot, "will be impossible."

King Hugo then declared he would summon the Royal Physician; or, if need be, scour the kingdom for alchemists, astrologers, midwives, village wonder-workers, whoever might transform her once again into human shape.

"That will be of no use," Margot said. "As you see me now, so shall I always be."

"Wretched girl!" King Hugo cried. "Do you mean to make a fool of me? What king ever had a cat for a daughter!"

"What cat ever had a king for a father?" Margot replied.

This only enraged King Hugo the more; and he swore, cat or no, she would receive her suitors and marry the first who was willing.

And so, when the Court Chamberlain came to announce the arrival of Duke Golo de Gobino, the King tried to compose himself and put the best face he could on the matter. For Golo, while hardly the cleverest, was the richest nobleman in the kingdom, with a purse as full as his head was empty. His estates lay beside those of the King; he had a fine regiment of cavalry, excellent stables and kennels, and his marriage to Elena would be all King Hugo ever could wish.

However, when Duke Golo saw the bejeweled Margot, his self-satisfied smile vanished, and he stammered in dismay:

"The Princess? She looks rather like a cat!"

"Pay it no mind," King Hugo said. "She's not quite herself today."

"So I see," replied Golo. "Indeed, I never would have recognized her. Whatever happened?"

"Nothing," said King Hugo. "A trivial indisposition, a minor ailment."

"But, Majesty," quavered Golo, "it may be contagious. Suppose I caught it from her. If I take her for my wife, the same could happen to me."

"In your case," said Margot, "it might be an advantage."

"Come now, Golo," the King insisted, "get on with it. She'll make you a fine wife."

"One thing's certain," added Margot, "you'll never be troubled with mice."

"Majesty," stammered Golo, "I came for your daughter's hand, not her paw."

"Golo!" bellowed the King. "I command you to marry her. Come back here!" But Duke Golo had already darted through the door and was making his way in all haste down the corridor.

King Hugo stormed at the cat for having lost him such a desirable son-in-law. But next came Count Bohamel de Braise, and the King once again tried to put a fair face on bad fortune. Though his estates were not as large as Golo's, Bohamel was a harsh overlord and what he lacked in land he made up in taxing his tenants; and, at this match, King Hugo would have been well satisfied.

However, when Count Bohamel saw Margot,

he threw back his head and gave a rasping laugh:

"Majesty, you make sport of me. Some wives have been called cats, but no cat's been called wife. Look at her claws! They'd tear the bedsheets to ribbons. If I ever dared embrace her, she'd scratch me to the bone."

"Your claws are sharper than mine," said Margot. "Ask your tenants."

No matter how King Hugo commanded or cajoled, pleaded or threatened, Bohamel would

have no part of marriage with a cat-princess.

"Your misfortune is your own, and not mine," he told the King, and strode from the chamber.

The same happened with the suitors who followed. Each, in turn, found one pretext or another:

"Good heavens, Majesty," protested the Marquis de Cabasson, shuddering. "With a wife like that, I could never invite my friends to dine. She'd never use the proper fork. And what a breach of etiquette when she drank from a saucer."

"I daresay your friends would be too deep in their cups," answered Margot, "to notice what I did with a saucer."

"A cat-wife?" sneered the Seigneur de Malcourir. "She'd dance on the rooftops with every passing tom."

"I assure you," said Margot, "my virtue's greater than yours."

By this time, word had spread through the palace that King Hugo's daughter had become a cat. The councillors and ministers gossiped, the court ladies tittered, the footmen snickered, the kitchen maids giggled; and soon all in the palace were whispering behind their hands or laughing up their sleeves.

"See what you've done!" cried the King. "Shamed me! Humiliated me!"

"How so?" asked Margot. "I'm not ashamed of being a cat. Are you ashamed of being a king?"

King Hugo threw himself down on a chair and held his head in his hands. Not only had his daughter turned into a cat, it was now plain to him she would also turn into a spinster; and instead of a profitable marriage, there would be none at all. He began groaning miserably, blaming his daughter's stubbornness for putting him in such a plight.

That moment, the Court Chamberlain announced the suitors had departed, all but one: Count Raimond.

"How dare he come here?" exclaimed the King. "He's as pigheaded as my daughter—no, no, I don't mean that. Go fetch him, then." He turned to Margot. "Let the fellow see for himself what you've done. You've outwitted yourself this time, my girl. Marry you? One look and he'll change his tune. But at any rate, I'll have seen the last of him."

Alarmed at this, it was all Princess Elena could do to keep silent in her hiding place. She had never expected Raimond to present himself at court, knowing her father would only refuse him. Now she remembered Margot's warning. If Raimond, too, believed her a cat, indeed her heart would break. Margot, sensing her anguish, dangled her tail over the edge of the couch and waved the tip like a cautioning finger.

The Chamberlain ushered in Count Raimond. To Elena, he had never looked handsomer nor had she loved him so much; and she burned to go to him then and there. But, worse than a broken heart was not knowing the strength of his love for her. So, tormented though she was, she bravely held her tongue.

At sight of the cat, Raimond halted. He stood silent a long moment before he said to

King Hugo:

"What I heard of Princess Elena I took for idle gossip. Now I see it is true."

With that, he stepped forward and bowed to Margot. Taking her paw in his hand, he said:

"Why, Princess, how well you look today. What a marvelous color your fur is. The stripes set it off to perfection. Your paws are softer than velvet. And what handsome whiskers, fine as threads of silk. You're beautiful as a cat as you were beautiful as a woman."

"What are you saying?" burst out King Hugo. "Have you gone mad? Paying court to a cat?"

"She's still my beloved as much as she's still your daughter," answered Raimond. "Do true lovers part because the hair of one goes white or the back of the other goes bent? Because the cheeks of one may wither, or the eyes of the other may dim? So long as her heart stays unchanged, so shall mine."

"Do you mean to tell me you'd marry her anyway?" cried King Hugo. "You, stand as bridegroom? And I, give her away? She'd make both of us look like fools."

"Majesty," said Raimond, "the only one who can make you look a fool is yourself. Yes, I will marry her if she will have it so. As for you, can it be that you love your daughter less than I love my intended? And yourself more than anyone else?"

At this, King Hugo began blustering and grumbling again. But, after a moment, he hung his head in shame. Finally, he said:

"My daughter is my daughter, whatever ill has befallen her; and I would have helped her least when she needed me the most. Well, Count of Albiclair, you're not the son-in-law I'd have chosen; but the choice was never mine in the first place. Marry, the two of you, if that's what you want. I still don't give a fig for your lute-plucking and verse-scribbling; but I do give you my blessing."

For her part, Elena was overjoyed at these words, and more than ever assured that Raimond was her true love. Again, she was about to leave her hiding place when, to her dismay, she heard Margot reply:

"Alas, there can be no wedding. Our marriage is out of the question."

"What do you mean?" roared King Hugo, now as determined to see his daughter wed Raimond as he had been against it. "You bedeviled me to give my consent. Now you have it."

"By your own decree, cats are against the law," said Margot. "How shall Raimond keep me as a wife when it's forbidden to keep a cat?"

"Blast the decree!" retorted the King. "That's the stupidest thing I ever heard of. I made that law, so I can change it. From this day

on, cats are welcome everywhere, even in my palace. In fact, I'll proclaim a new law that all my subjects must obey: Everyone must keep a cat."

"No, Majesty," answered Margot. "Only let cats freely choose their people, and people choose their cats, and we shall get along very well."

At this, Princess Elena sprang from under the couch and threw her arms around the bewildered but joyful Raimond. And King Hugo commanded all the bells to be rung for the

betrothal of the two lovers.

Instead of being angry at Margot for having tricked him, King Hugo kept his word, and better. He invited every cat in the kingdom to the wedding; and set out for them tables laden with bowls of cream, platters of fish and fowl, and bouquets of catnip. And Margot, as Maid of Honor, carried the bride's train.

King Hugo also repealed his other foolish laws. Though he grew no fonder of pickled herrings or holidays, he never again forbade them to his subjects. And because he saw to it that all cats were treated with utmost respect, he became known throughout the land as Hugo the Cat-King, a title which hardly pleased him but which he accepted nevertheless.

In gratitude, the Princess would have kept Margot in silks and jewels; but the cat politely declined, saying she was quite comfortable in her own fur. While she stayed with Elena and Raimond happily all their lives, having seen the ways of kings and courtiers, Margot privately judged it far more sensible to be a cat.

A Valentine's Day Poem

MIRIAM CHAIKIN

There was nothing from you
on Valentine's Day,
no card, no note, not even a call.

Same thing last year.
I don't care; not a bit,
just happened to notice—that's all.

Here's a card from me,
made it up myself,
and taped it to the door of your house.
    Undear unfriend,
    I hereby unsend
    unValentine wishes to you, you louse.
    THE END

My Valentine

ROBERT LOUIS STEVENSON

I will make you brooches and toys for your delight
Of bird song at morning and starshine at night.
I will make a palace fit for you and me,
   Of green days in forests
   And blue days at sea.

Giraffes

MARY ANN HOBERMAN

I like them.
Ask me why.
    Because they hold their heads so high.
    Because their necks stretch to the sky.
    Because they're quiet, calm, and shy.
    Because they run so fast they fly.
    Because their eyes are velvet brown.
    Because their coats are spotted tan.
    Because they eat the tops of trees.
    Because their legs have knobby knees.
    Because
    Because
    Because. That's why
I like giraffes.

73

From
Love
Song

ARNOLD ADOFF

Chocolate
Chocolate
              i
love
      you so
              i
want
        to
marry
        you
        and
live
      forever
              in the
                flavor
of your
   brown

Make Yourself, and Your Valentine, a Holiday Sweet

Candy is the traditional Valentine gift. These are easy to make. Try not to eat them all before you give them to your friend.

Chocolate Cherries

You need:

1 jar of maraschino cherries with stems

5 squares of semi-sweet chocolate (available in the baking section of the grocery store)

How to:

Drain the juice from the cherries. Melt the chocolate in a double boiler. Remove the chocolate from the stove. Dip the cherries into the melted chocolate and place on waxed paper. Let the cherries cool. Give the candy to your Valentine. You scrape the chocolate pot and give yourself a Valentine treat.

Does She Love Me? Does He Love Me?

People have been using fruit, flowers, and games for years to find out if they are loved. Try some of these that your great-great-grandparents probably tried when they were your age.

Does He Or She Love You?

The Daisy

This will work with any flower that has petals, but it is traditionally done with a daisy. Pluck the petals one by one from the flower. As you pull each petal, alternate saying, "He loves me" and "He loves me not." The last remaining petal will tell you if he indeed does love you. Yes. You can find out if she loves you the same way.

Who Will You Marry?

The Apple Stem

Think of five or six names of boys or girls you might marry. As you twist the stem of an apple, recite the names until the stem comes off. You will marry the person whose name you were saying when the stem fell off.

How Old Will You Be When You Marry?

Ball Bouncing

Bounce a ball on the sidewalk. Count as you bounce. The number you have counted when you miss will tell you how old you will be when you get married. Better practice bouncing a ball, or you may end up marrying when you are three years old.

How Long Will You Stay Married?

Jumping Rope

Take your jump rope outside and jump for love. Count as you jump. When you miss, the number will tell you how many years you will be married.

How Many Children Will You Have?

The Dandelion

Pick a dandelion that has gone to seed. Take a deep breath and blow the seeds into the wind. Count the seeds that remain on the stem. That is the number of children you will have.

Apple Seeds

If you cut an apple in half and count how many seeds are inside, you will also know how many children you will have.

Did you eever, iver, over

TRADITIONAL

Did you eever, iver, over,
In your leef, life, loaf,
See the deevel, divel, dovel,
Kiss his weef, wife, woaf?

No, I neever, niver, nover,
In my leef, life, loaf,
Saw the deevel, divel, dovel,
Kiss his weef, wife, woaf.

The Lizzie Pitofsky Poem

JUDITH VIORST

I can't get enoughsky
Of Lizzie Pitofsky.
I love her so much that it hurts.
I want her so terrible
I'd give her my gerbil
Plus twenty-two weeks of desserts.

I know that it's lovesky
'Cause Lizzie Pitofsky
Is turning me into a saint.
I smell like a rose,
I've stopped picking my nose,
And I practically never say ain't.

80

I don't push and shovesky
'Cause Lizzie Pitofsky
Likes boys who are gentle and kind.
I'm not throwing rocks
And I'm changing my socks
(And to tell you the truth I don't mind).

Put tacks in my shoes,
Feed me vinegar juice,
And do other mean bad awful stuffsky.
But promise me this:
I won't die without kiss-
Ing my glorious Lizzie Pitofsky.

The Valentine

MICHAEL PATRICK HEARN

Who sent me this?
I wish I knew,
But all it says
Is just "GUESS WHO?"
It might be Cindy
In the second row,
Mindy or Lindy—
I just don't know!
Maybe it's Rita—
No, I must be nuts!
She told my sister
That she hates my guts!
Could it be Emily,
Rebecca or Kayleigh,
Elysia or Hayley,
Caroline, Marilyn,
Tawana or Donna,
Colleen, Aileen, Irene, Helene,

Hilary or Valery,
Maybe Mona or Mary,
Martha, Minnie, Melanie,
Or Malory,
Molly or Matty,
Holly or Hattie,
Polly or Patty—
I wish I knew!
Now let me think—
Could it be
  YOU?

"I Love You"
Around the World

AMERICAN SIGN LANGUAGE:

ARABIC: احبتّى (Anah be-HEB-BEK)

CHINESE: 我愛你 (woh I nee)

EGYPTIAN, ANCIENT: 𓌻𓂋𓄿𓏏𓅱 Mer-a tù

FRENCH: Je t'aime (zhuh TEMM)

GERMAN: Ich liebe dich (ikh LEE-buh dikh)

HEBREW: אני אוהב אותך (ah-NEE o HEV O-TAKH)

ITALIAN: Io t'amo (ee-oh tah-moh)

JAPANESE: 私は貴女を愛しています。 (wah-TAH-SHEE-WAH
ah-NAH-TAH-OH-AH- eesh-tay ee-mas)

RUSSIAN: Я тебя люблю (ya te-BYA lyoo-BLYOO)

SPANISH: Yo te amo (yoh tay AH-moh)

SWAHILI: Mimi nakupenda (mee-mee na-koo-pen-da)

Read About Valentine's Day

Index

Something to Read

Arthur's Great Big Valentine by Lillian Hoban. Art by the author. HarperCollins. *Valentine's Day isn't fun if you've had a fight with your best friend.*

Arthur's Valentine by Marc Brown. Art by the author. Atlantic–Little Brown. *Who is Arthur's secret admirer?*

The Best Valentine in the World by Marjorie Weinman Sharmat. Art by Lilian Obligado. Holiday House. *Ferdinand Fox makes a purple valentine for Florette.*

Carry Go Bring Come by Vyanne Samuels. Art by Jennifer Northway. Four Winds. *Leon's sister is getting married, and the whole family wants Leon to run errands for them.*

Four Valentines in a Rainstorm by Felicia Bond. Art by the author. HarperCollins. *When it rains hearts, Cornelia makes valentines.*

One Zillion Valentines by Frank Modell. Art by the author. Greenwillow. *Marvin and Milton make valentines for everyone in the neighborhood.*

The Owl and the Pussycat by Edward Lear. Art by Jan Brett. Putnam. *The Owl and the Pussycat were married and they "danced by the light of the moon, the moon, they danced by the light of the moon."*

Rosebud and Red Flannel by Ethel Pochocki. Art by Mary

Beth Owens. Holt. *Love in a winter snowstorm.*

Rosie and Michael by Judith Viorst. Art by Lorna Tomei. Atheneum. *Rosie and Michael are best friends, no matter what. . . .*

The Valentine Bears by Eve Bunting. Art by Jan Brett. Clarion. *Mr. Bear vows to wake up from his winter sleep to celebrate Valentine's Day with Mrs. Bear.*

Valentine's Day by Gail Gibbons. Art by the author. Holiday House. *The origins and customs of Valentine's Day.*

LONGER BOOKS

Alice in Rapture, Sort Of by Phyllis Reynolds Naylor. Atheneum. *Alice's father calls it "the summer of the first boyfriend."*

All for Love edited by Tasha Tudor. Art by the editor. Philomel. *Poems, love letters, legends, songs, and recipes.*

Bingo Brown and the Language of Love by Betsy Byars. Viking. *Bingo is in love with Melissa, but she has moved far away.*

Cupid and Psyche: A Love Story by Edna Barth. Art by Ati Forberg. Seabury. *The Greek god of love falls in love with a beautiful young girl. A Greek myth.*

Dagmar Schultz and the Angel Edna by Lynn Hall. Scribners. *Dagmar's guardian angel, Aunt Edna, has a "no boyfriends" rule.*

Merry Ever After by Joe Lasker. Art by the author. Viking. *The story of a noble wedding and a peasant wedding in medieval Europe.*

Romeo and Juliet—Together (and Alive!) at Last by Avi. Orchard. *The way to get two shy people together is to cast them as great lovers in a class play.*

Index

Adoff, Arnold, 74

Alexander, Lloyd, 51

. . . *And Then the Prince Knelt Down and Tried to Put the Glass Slipper on Cinderella's Foot*, 48

Be My Non-Valentine, 16

Cassedy, Sylvia, 43

Cat-King's Daughter, The, 51

Chaikin, Miriam, 71

Conversation Hearts, 3

Did you eever, iver, over, 79

Ellie's Valentine, 21

February, 14

Fisher, Aileen, 4

Giovanni, Nikki, 41

Giraffes, 73

Greenfield, Eloise, 5

Hearn, Michael Patrick, 82

Here It Is, 38

Hill, Mildred J., 18

Hoberman, Mary Ann, 73

Hug Me, 9

Hughes, Langston, 42

I like bugs, 40

Joans, Ted, 15

Katz, Bobbi, 17

Krauss, Ruth, 7

Kuskin, Karla, 6, 40

Lizzie Pitofsky Poem, The, 80

Love Don't Mean, 5
Love Song, 74
Love Tight, 15
Making Sandwich-Kisses, 7
Merriam, Eve, 16, 47
My Valentine, 72
Parks, Gordon, 46
Paulsen, Linda G., 14
Payne, Nina, 3
Poem, 42
Porcupine, The, 6
Private Valentines, 17
Rylant, Cynthia, 21
Short Love Poem, 13

Stevenson, Robert Louis, 72
Stren, Patti, 9
Turner, Ann, 38
two friends, 41
Valentine, The, 82
Valentine To My Puppy, A, 37
Valentines, 4
Valentine's Day Poem, A, 71
Viorst, Judith, 13, 48, 80
When, 47
When You Send a Valentine, 18
X X X X X, 43
Yolen, Jane, 37
You are, 46